CATCHER

DAVE ABBOTT

Inisfree Communications
Vancouver, B.C.

Distributed by **Gordon Soules Book
Publishers Ltd.** ● 1359 Ambleside Lane,
West Vancouver, BC, Canada V7T 2Y9
● PMB 620, 1916 Pike Place #12,
Seattle, WA 98101-1097 US
E-mail: books@gordonsoules.com
Web site: http://www.gordonsoules.com
(604) 922 6588 Fax: (604) 688 5442

First edition: October 1999
Second edition: January 2000

Canadian Cataloguing in Publication Data

Abbott, Dave
Catch the Irish Laughter
ISBN 0-9686024-0-1

1. Humour – Authorship, I. Title. II.
TX644.C65 1999 808'.066641 C99-910708-3

Innisfree Communications
14 Sennok Crescent, Vancouver, B.C.
Canada V6N 2E4

Typesetting and Design by
Cardinal Communications
Vancouver, B.C. V6P 2W9

This book has been set in
Garamond 12 pt.

Printed in Canada by
Hignell Printing Ltd.
Winnipeg, Manitoba R3B 2B4

Dedication

To my wife Diane, for her love,
support and laughter.
And to my daughter Ingrid and her children,
Hilary and Nicholas
to celebrate their Irish heritage.

Thanks

To Monika Forberger for her commitment and patience; Gerry Gawne of Seattle for his inspiration and enthusiasm and Maura McCay, publisher of *The Celtic Connection* newspaper for her ongoing support and participation.

Table of Contents

Slainte/Welcome

W elcome to a smidgen of wit and a tincture of the wisdom of the Irish. A collection of stories, anecdotes, and humour in the Irish tradition.

Ireland is a land in which comedy, humour and wit are deeply ingrained in the national character and remain an essential ingredient in people's daily lives. You'll find it in the wit and thrust of their everyday conversation.

There's a delight in wordplay and mischief, a rapture in the telling and embellishing of a good story and the sheer malicious glee of the Irish national pastime of 'slagging' -- a basic philosophy of humorously criticising or insulting someone for the sheer sport of it.

In Ireland it seems anyone is capable of coming up with a remark that can haunt the victim for life. A few years ago a member of the Irish parliament described the Minister of Finance's contribution to the economic debate as "having managed to subtract from the sum total of human knowledge."

Dethroning the pompous and a shared delight in satire, parody and the grotesque (especially the grotesque) can be traced back in an unbroken line for more than a thousand years.

For example: here's the story of two IRA guys driving a car on their way to plant a bomb outside a British Army barracks, and one says to the other, "For God's sake slow down Paddy, for this is a dreadful bumpy road and the bomb in the back seat might go off."

"Aah," says Paddy, "sure don't worry Mick, didn't I put a spare in the trunk."

And with the grotesque there was always a belief in magic, for the Irish have a penchant for fantasy, fairies and hidden supernatural forces that remains alive in the Irish imagination and has helped set them apart. For example I assume you heard that "St. Patrick drove all the snakes out of Ireland."

George Bernard Shaw defined an Irishman's heart as his 'imagination' which, if true, is an imagination that enlightened and entertained millions throughout the world. — a world which has happily embraced W.B. Yeats, Oscar Wilde and such diverse talents as The Abbey Theatre, The Chieftains, Maeve Binchy and Riverdance, to name a few!

Add names like Barry Fitzgerald, Maureen O'Hara and Liam Neeson, and poets like Paddy Kavanagh (heir to William Butler Yeats) and you have a country in which eccentricity is not only appreciated but also celebrated.

As a young boy living in the Dublin of the 1940s and

1950s I recall the city's squalid slums and the extreme poverty on the streets. Many of Dublin's once elegant Georgian houses overflowed with large families unable to afford the upkeep, and thus the houses had fallen into disrepair. Children were dressed in rags, many were barefoot. If they didn't die of malnutrition then they'd likely die of consumption, the "Catholic disease" as it was known to the absentee English landlords.

Frank McCourt set his Pulitzer-prize-winning book *Angela's Ashes* in Limerick, but his description of the housing, schooling and the hard scrabble for existence was true of almost any town in Ireland a few decades earlier.

It was about this time when tourists and visitors started to arrive in noticeable numbers. The majority of them enjoyed the locals, finding them delightfully odd, eccentric and classically Celt, namely unmanageable --drunk or sober!

On the other hand, visitors from Britain were frequently distrustful of the Irish, which one can understand when one considers the English ruling class believed for centuries that "every Irishman has a potato in his head and they are little more than a race of blaspheming bog-trotting drunks, lazy, cunning and untrustworthy."

But, in due course, they discovered that Erin's green isle was indeed green and a land where no one is a stranger but only a friend one has yet to meet.

The attitude of foreigner visitors was part historical, part propaganda mixed with ignorance, for the Irish had always been the underclass in England, Canada and Australia. It was especially so in the United States in earlier times when the Irish were chosen to clear the malarial swamps, being lower in value than the black slaves who worked the plantations, and therefore expendable.

For decades, Irish women attempting to escape starvation in Ireland ended up as either maids or prostitutes in England. Irish men who emigrated were frequently rejected and considered unworthy to associate with being, for the most part, Catholic, poor, and uneducated.

Then the American tourists started appearing in ever-increasing numbers on the streets of Dublin, guidebooks in hand, wearing enormous hats and high heels, wrapped in fur coats, heavily perfumed, with large rings on manicured hands and dangling gold necklaces hanging from their necks – and those were the men!

The tourists were exotic creatures and regarded as the rarest of hothouse flowers for they were known as glamorous, kind and insatiably curious.

Ireland is also a land where a visitor should hesitate
before asking directions for they may become even more
confused when they are actually given the directions.
Like the old codger I met on a country road who,
when I asked him how I could get to Tipperary, pointed
his finger imperiously down the road towards a distant sign
and said, "D'ye see that sign?"

I said, " Yes, yes"

He asked again, "D'ye see it now?"

"Yes. Yes, quite clearly," I said expectantly, at which
point he pronounced,

"Well, don't take that one!"

Or like the old josser in Galway who, when I asked if
this was the right road to Donegal said, "Well now, to tell
you the truth sir, if I was going to Donegal I wouldn't have
started from here."

Sir Peter Ustinov told me his favourite Irish story
occurred when he returned to Dublin following an ab-
sence of three months, to make yet another movie. He was
greeted by the hotel doorman who said, "Aah, Mr Ustinov,
I'm so glad to see you for I never got a chance to say
good-bye." And then as he walked to his room the bellhop
said, "Follow me Sir Peter, I'll be right behind you!"

Of course some Americans were viewed as loud, self-confident and bold. Especially Texans who, as we know, like to claim Texas is the biggest place in the world.

I recall once hearing about a Texas rancher who, upon meeting a County Cork farmer boasted, " It takes me a whole damn day to drive from one side of my ranch to the other!"

The Corkman looked at him and said, "Aah sure I know how that can be sir, we have tractors like that over here too."

There is another aspect to the Irish character you may recognise. The Irish love to talk. Maybe you've noticed? They talk when they're sad; they talk about being sorta sad, nearly sad, not quite sad. They talk when they're drunk, or getting drunk, when they've been drunk, and before getting drunk. The one thing they will not talk about is sex.

Sex education was a thousand dirty jokes told on street corners and was too sinful ever to be romantic. It was strictly for procreation, with the entire process remaining secretive and mysterious

A child bold enough to ask about sex was told that "babies were found under cabbages," which was immediately followed by warnings that if you "touch yerself, you'll go blind," or the even more terrifying "you'll grow hair on your palms." The result was that thousands of young Irish boys spent hours examining their hands looking for hair on their palms.

Adolescence and puberty was an agonizing time. American writer Naomi Wolf in her book *Promiscuities* wrote "Our sexual histories are often tapestries stitched around great areas of silence." She could have been writing of Ireland, where that silence was deafening.

Dammed by the Church, unwed mothers brought everlasting shame on the family so most of them were hastily packed off to England for an abortion where many died. Those choosing to remain behind in Ireland often ended up working in the local convent as virtual slaves.

For boys it was somewhat different. Many Irish mothers considered it a mark of honour and prestige to have a son a priest since it virtually guaranteed her a place in heaven

Disobey the local priest and severe penalties — both in this life and the next — awaited those who committed sins of the flesh. The all-powerful Catholic Church relied on celibacy, chastity and abstinence, along with the twin pillars of fear and ignorance, for its power base.

It is true Ireland never suffered the horrors of a world war, yet it has a catalogue of disasters that is fairly comprehensive. Eight hundred years of British occupation, uprisings, insurrections, political and social disunity, plus the twin holocausts of famine and mass emigration.

In recent times there have been thirty years of violence in the North, not to mention the stifling power of the Catholic Church which, happily, today has greatly declined.

It is hard to realise, when one views the prosperity Ireland is enjoying today, that the island nation has only been a republic for 70 years.

Cut loose from the British after centuries of exploitation, it was left with no city, industry or a market for its products. That situation has radically changed since Ireland became a member of the European Union and leapfrogged into the 21st century. Today Ireland is considered the "Tiger of Europe." Interestingly, Ireland has little or no philosophical tradition. Reality is grasped largely not through ideas, but through stories.

A man or a woman is a story. His or her history is a story. As one writer put it, "I love the Irish, they are great liars, they're the best company in the world, and the makers of stories." Or as poet Brendan Kennelly will tell you, "a good story puts a shape on the incomprehensible."

But Ireland's greatest export has been people, with an estimated 70 million of Irish extraction living around the

14

world today. Forty-five million Americans and eight million Canadians lay claim to Irish ancestry

The Irish share a rich heritage in the United States, Canada and Australia and appear everywhere — sometimes in the most unexpected places and often where they ought not to be. Their contributions have yet to be fully documented, for their achievements and contributions to the world are disproportionate to their numbers.

Ireland remains a country inhabited by a race that seems to move back in time, to *Tir-na-Og*, the land of the ever young.

I hope you enjoy this book and will visit Ireland to meet the people who tell these stories. There you will find a hundred thousand welcomes awaiting you – *Cead mile failte.*

David Abbott,
Vancouver, B.C.
Canada

Have you heard the one about . . . ?

The Seannacai, or story teller, plays an important role in Ireland. The teller of stories was the chronicler, the historian, the communicator from time immemorial. To tell a story well is considered an art form in Ireland. Share a story in Ireland and tell it well and you will be admired and welcome anywhere. I hope you will enjoy these uniquely Irish stories.

Two nuns, riding in a small red mini car, went shopping at a supermarket in Co. Kerry, but couldn't find a place to park.

One nun said to the other, "You go in and get the groceries and I'll keep driving around until you come out."

But when she came out of the supermarket, she couldn't find the nun or the car. She went over to Flanagan, who was standing outside the store, and asked him, "Have you seen a nun in a red Mini?"

"No," he replied seriously, "not since I took the pledge."

Paddy Maloney was captain of a jet, and one day he made the following announcement to the waiting passengers:

"Ladies and gentlemen, sorry for the long delay in the take off. I'm delighted to report that we don't have a bomb on board, as we first feared. At least, if we have, we haven't been able to find it."

♣

Q. How do you recognize a Mick in Las Vegas?
A. He's the one playing the stamp machine.

♣

A 96-year-old Irishman was taken to the hospital after he hurt himself chasing a couple of young girls around his house. After doing the same thing to the nurses in the hospital for several weeks he finally gave up the ghost. But he was smiling when he died.

Two of his old mates came to the wake.

"Jaysus, he looks badly failed."

"What did you expect?" said the other, "Him only just after coming out of the hospital."

Pat was in a fit of depression and one night Bridget came home to find him standing on a chair with a rope around his waist.

"What the hell are you doing?" she demanded.

"I'm committing suicide," Pat replied.

"Then why haven't you got the rope around your neck?"

"Well, I had," said Pat, "but it was choking me."

♣

Written on notice of death certificate:

Went to bed feeling on top of the world, but when he woke up he was dead.

♣

Three sailors – and Englishman, a Scotsman and an Irishman — are washed up on the shores of an island inhabited by cannibals. They are caught and brought to the chief of the tribe.

The chief says to the first, "Where are you from?"

"England."

"Into the pot" says the chief.

"Where are you from?" he asks the second sailor.

"Scotland, sir."

"Into the pot" commands the chief.

"And, where are you from?" he asks the paddy.

"Ireland sir, yer honour."

"You leave – go back on the boat."

As the Irishman was leaving he said, "Excuse me chief, why did you not put me in the pot with the others?"

"Last time we put an Irishman in the pot he ate all the potatoes."

♣

"You are charged," said the judge to Pat, "with having wilfully, feloniously and with malice aforethought appropriated to your own use and behoof a certain article, to wit, a bovine quadruped; the aforementioned quadruped having been wrongfully and feloniously abstracted by you from the state of one Daniel Murphy on or about the fourth day of July anno domini 1887 contrary to the law of the land. How do you plead?

"Not guilty, your honour," said Pat. "Sure all I did was steal a cow."

An Irish Mother's Letter to her Son

This classic letter has been around for as long as I can remember, and is one of my favourites. It comes with many variations and in various forms, but the P.S. is always the same.

MacGillicuddy Reeks,

Co. Cork

Dear Son,

Just a few lines to let you know that I'm still alive. I'm writing this letter slowly because I know you can't read very quickly. You won't know the house when you come home because we've moved.

About your father, he has a lovely job with 500 men under him – he's cutting the grass at the cemetery. Your brother Sean is doing well in the Army. He's only been a soldier for two weeks, and they've already made him a Court-Martial.

There was a washing machine in the new house when we moved, but it isn't working too good; last week I put 14 shirts in it, pulled the chain and haven't seen them since.

Mary, your sister, has had her baby, but I don't know whether it's a boy or a girl, so I can't tell if you you're an aunt or an uncle.

Your Uncle Seamus drowned in a vat of whiskey in the brewery. Some of his work mates dived in to save him, but he fought them off bravely. We cremated his body, and it took four days to put the fire out.

It only rained twice last week, once for three days, and once for four days. Monday was so windy that one chicken laid the same egg five times.

We had a letter from the undertaker. He said if the last instalment wasn't paid within seven days on your grand-mother's funeral – up she comes!

Your loving mother

P.S. I was going to send you five pounds, but I've already sealed the envelope.

Leaving Home

*The Irish have been "leaving home" for hundreds of years, and are
thus scattered all over the world. Victims of famine, repression and
cruelty, millions sought safety and greener pastures overseas, often
dying in the attempt. Thousands were sent to penal colonies in
Australia and the United States. Many became priests, nuns and
missionaries and served overseas. Emigrants like me sought opportu-
nities abroad in the 1950s and 1960s when Ireland was still strug-
gling to provide for those who remained. Here are some of the stories
that have become part of the folklore of the Irish abroad.*

Dear Father and Mother,

Pen cannot dictate the poverty of this country at
present. The potato crop is quite done away with all over
Ireland. There is nothing expected here, only an immediate
famine. If you knew the danger we and our fellow countrymen are suffering, if you were ever so much distressed,
you would take us out of this poverty isle . . . For God's
sake take us out of poverty and don't let us die of hunger.

Letter from Mary Rush, County Sligo
To her parents in Quebec, 1846

The last embraces were terrible to see; but worse were the kissings and claspings of the hands during the long minutes we remained . . . We became aware for the first time perhaps of the full dignity of that civilisation which induces control of the expression of emotions . . . All the while that this lamentation was giving me a headache . . . there could not but be a feeling that these people, thus giving vent to their instincts, were as children, and would command themselves better when they were wiser.

English journalist's description of Irish family about to be permanently separated by migration to America. From Harriet Martinea, Letters from Ireland, 1852

[In America] the labourer can earn as much in one day as will support him for a week. The richest land in the world may be purchased here . . . for $1.25 an acre – equal to 5s 3d . . . If I could show them [in Ireland] the splendid prairie I am looking on, extending in wild luxuriant verdure as far as the eye can reach – how different would their situation be from what it is! How gladly they would fly with their families!

Letter from an Irish immigrant Name unknown, January 1848

Penal Colonists to Politicians

During the Ireland disorders of 1848, nine young men were captured, tried and convicted of treason against the Queen. Their sentence was death.

The presiding judge read out the (names of) the condemned: Charles Duffy, Morris Leyne, Patrick Donahue, Thomas McGee, John Mitchel, Thomas Meagher, Richard O'Gorman, Terence McManus and Michael Ireland.

"Have you anything to say before the Court passes sentence?" asked the judge.

Thomas Meagher had been chosen to speak for them.

"My Lord, this is our first offence, but not our last. If you will be easy with us this once we promise, on our word as gentlemen, to try to do better next time. And the next time we won't be fools enough to get caught."

The indignant judge sentenced them to be hanged by the neck, but passionate protests from all over the world forced Queen Victoria to commute the sentences. The men were to be transported for life to the penal colonies of the then savage Australia.

In 1877, a Sir Charles Duffy was elected Prime Minister of the Australian State of Victoria. To her amazement, Queen Victoria learned that this was the same Charles

Duffy who had been transported for high treason 20 years before.

She demanded the records of the other men who had been exiled, and this is what she learned.

Meagher was Governor of Montana; McManus and Donahue were brigadier generals in the U.S. Army. O'Gorman was the Governor-General of Newfoundland; Morris Leyne had been Attorney-General of Australia, to which office Michael succeeded; McGee was president of the Council for the Dominion of Canada; Mitchel was a prominent New York politician, who later became father of the Mitchel who was mayor of New York.

From the Evening Herald, Dublin

The Importance of Being Oscar

O scar Fingall O'Flahertie Wills Wilde was born in Dublin to parents of considerable importance.

His father, Sir William Wilde, was knighted as an internationally famous eye doctor and surgeon.

His mother, Lady Jane Wilde, nee Elgee, was twenty-eight when Oscar was born. She was a tall, stately, imposing woman – talented and eccentric. She wrote under the nom-de-plume of "Speranza" and was a clever talker. Oscar resembled her in looks, voice and eccentricities.

In his youth he had a young man's normal interest in girls. When he married he was passionately in love with his wife, and once caused acute embarrassment to a friend by describing in unnecessary detail the physical pleasures of his marriage.

Women later ceased to attract him, and in 1889, he commenced the course of conduct that led to his eventual downfall.

Oscar Wilde died on 30 November 1900, of cerebral meningitis.

Wilde's Witticisms

Work is the curse of the drinking class.

♣

One of those characteristic British faces that, once seen, are never remembered.

♣

The English have a miraculous power of turning wine into water.

♣

Whenever I think of my bad qualities at night, I go to sleep at once.

♣

He is old enough to know worse.

♣

Nowadays most people die of a sort of creeping common sense, and discover when it is too late that the only things one never regrets are one's mistakes.

Consistency is the last refuge of the unimaginative. Whenever a man does a thoroughly stupid thing, it is always from the noblest motives.

♣

Morality is simply the attitude we adopt towards people whom we personally dislike.

♣

I choose my friends for their good looks, my acquaintances for their good characters, and my enemies for their good intellects. A man cannot be too careful in the choice of his enemies.

♣

To win back my youth there is nothing I would not do – nothing. Except take up exercise, get up early, or be a useful member of the community.

♣

I never put off till tomorrow what I can possibly do the day after.

There is no secret to life. Life's aim, if it has one, is simply to be always looking for temptations. There are not nearly enough of them. I sometimes pass a whole day without coming across a single one. It is quite dreadful. It makes one so nervous about the future.

♣

Twenty years of romance make a woman look like a ruin; but twenty years of marriage make her something like a public building.

♣

It is sad. One half of the world does not believe in God, and the other half does not believe in me.

♣

A cynic is the man who knows the price of everything and the value of nothing.

♣

Each class preaches the importance of those virtues it need not exercise. The rich harp on the value of thrift, the idle grow eloquent over the dignity of labour.

♣

The tragedy of old age is not that one is old, but that one is young.

♣

One should always be in love. That is the reason one should never marry.

♣

To love oneself is the beginning of a life-long romance.

♣

Men always want to be a woman's first love. That is their clumsy vanity. Women have a more subtle instinct about things: What they like is to be a man's last romance.

♣

It is quite remarkable how one good action always breeds another.

♣

In England people actually try to be brilliant at breakfast. That is so dreadful of them! Only dull people are brilliant at breakfast.

The Americans are certainly great hero worshippers, and they always take their heroes from the criminal classes.

♣

I like talking to a brick wall. It's the only thing in the world that never contradicts me.

♣

I do like talking to myself. It saves time and prevents arguments.

♣

I hate people who talk about themselves .when one wants to talk about oneself .

♣

When people agree with me, I always feel that I must be wrong.

♣

The old believe everything; the middle-aged suspect everything; the young know everything.

♣

To get back one's youth, one has merely to repeat one's follies.

32

Each class preaches the importance of those virtues it need not exercise. The rich harp on the value of thrift, the idle grow eloquent over the dignity of labour.

♣

Young men want to be faithful and are not; old men want to be faithless, and cannot.

♣

I am dying beyond my means (Wilde on drinking champagne on his deathbed).

More Words on Wilde

Oscar Wilde had both supporters and detractors in the England of his day. Here are a few examples showing the esteem in which his literary peers held him.

George Bernard Shaw

Wilde and I got on extraordinarily well on this occasion. I had not to talk myself, but to listen to a man telling me stories better than I could have told them . . . And he had an audience on whom not one of his subtlest effects was lost. And so for once our meeting was a success; and I understood why Morris (James), when he was dying, enjoyed a visit from Wilde more than from anyone else.

James Joyce (on Oscar's detractors)

His detractors . . . an imperfectly warm-blooded race, apparently conceive him as a great white caterpillar.

Dorothy Parker, writing on his mastery of the epigram:

> If, with the literate, I am
> Impelled to make an epigram,
> I never seek to take the credit;
> We all assume that Oscar said it.

The Saints Preserve Us

The Saints are integral part of everyday life in Ireland. There is a Saint for every day of the year, and for every charitable cause. Special Saint days were observed with great solemnity and accorded great respect.

Mother Superior was asking three young ladies graduating from high school what they were going to do with their lives.

The first one replied that she was going to take the veil and stay in the nunnery with the Mother Superior. The second said she was going to teach children in a good Catholic school. When she asked the third one, the young girl stated "I'm going to be a prostitute." Mother Superior shrieked and fainted to the floor. They quickly revived her. Mother Superior gasped. "Eileen, say that again."

"I'm going to a prostitute!" said the girl.

"Oh, Saints preserve us," she said, crossing herself quickly, "I thought you said a Protestant."

A young couple, Pat and Mary moved to a new town and visited the local parish priest who told them they'd be welcome in his church providing they abstained from sex for two weeks.

"Now yis understand" says Father Flanagan, "there's to be no intimacy for two weeks." The young couple agreed and off they went. Two weeks later they returned.

"So how's did yis do?" asks Father Flanagan "did ye do without the sex for the two weeks?"

"Well, not exactly, Father," says the young man. "Ye see, we were abstainin' right up until yesterday when, as Mary was reaching up to the top shelf for a can of tea didn't she spill it all over the ground.

So when she gets down on all fours to sweep it up I couldn't resist, and I took her right there and then, Father, on the floor. I'm very sorry, Father, very sorry."

"Well, says the priest "you're not welcome in my church."

To which the young man replied

"Aah, that's o.k. Father, sure we're not welcome at the Safeway either."

Mick Muldoon went to confession: "Bless me Father, for I have sinned. I have been with a loose woman from the congregation"

The priest replies, " Is that you Mick Muldoon?"

"Yes, Father it is."

"Who was the woman you were with?"

"I can't remember her name, Father"

"Was it Bridget O'Toole?"

"No, I don't think so, Father"

"Was it Patsy O'Donnell ?"

"No, Father"

"Was it Mary Murphy ?"

"No Father"

"Very well. Paddy Say five Our Fathers and two Hail Marys."

Outside the church, Mick's brother Sean was waiting

"What did you get?" he asked.

"Five Our Fathers, two Hail Marys and three good leads!"

♣

Pat was complimenting the priest after a particularly fine piece of preaching.

"That sermon Father," he said to him, "was like a drink of water to a drowning man."

A man enters a monastery where he has to take a vow of silence. He is allowed to communicate only once every five years, and then only in three words or less. Five years pass and the head abbot brings him into his office. He asks,

"Have you anything to say?"

The monk replies, "Bed too hard."

The abbot nods and sends the monk back to his work.

Another five years pass and again the monk is invited to speak with the abbot.

This time the monk says, "Food bad."

The abbot nods and the monk returns to his work.

Yet another five years pass in silence and once again the monk is invited to make known anything he wishes to communicate.

"I quit," says the monk.

"I'm not surprised," replies the abbot, "you've done nothing but complain since the day you got here."

There's the story of the Irish priest who was a bit mixed up and sought counselling. He was sent to see a famous psychiatrist who told him to forget his parish and his flock and take a trip to London and really enjoy himself for a few days.

"Take off your dog collar," the shrink recommended, "let your hair down and have a good time."

The priest did just that – he went to London and took off his dog collar. He saw a movie and had a wonderful meal, and a drop of the hard stuff.

Later that evening he found himself in Soho, in one of the "clip joints". He sat down at a table and a topless waitress came up and murmured,

"What would you like to drink, Father?"

The priest panicked, and thought he must have left his collar on by mistake. He stuttered to the waitress,

"How did you know I was a priest?"

"Oh, I'm Sister Theresa. I go to the same psychiatrist."

The Irish Abroad

Do you remember when the United Nations requested an Irish battalion be sent to the Congo in Africa to keep the peace after the civil war there?

There was the Irish UN contingent lined up in the hot dusty dry square in Leopoldville and the sergeant was addressing the men.

"Men" he says, "now yis are gathered here to fight these black fellas. Now these black fellas fight strange. They fight with bows and arrows but the end of the arrows is loaded with poison and if that hits ye in the arm ye'll be dead unless you do as yis are told. Pluck the arrow outta yer arm, don't mind your shirt, ye can get another tomorrow free from stores, put yer mouth down, suck like hell and spit out.

Now men, remember that. Suck like hell and spit out! Are there any questions?" A hand went up at the back of the line.

"Oh, it's you O'Reilly, what d'you want?"

" I want to know, Sergeant, what happens if I get one of them arrows in my arse?"

To which the Sergeant replied, "O'Reilly, that's when you'll know who your true friends are!"

A rabbi and an Irish priest were alone together in the carriage of a train. After a while, the priest opened the conversation by saying, "I know that in your religion you are not supposed to eat pork. Have you actually ever tasted it?"

The rabbi said, "I must tell the truth. Yes I have, on the odd occasion."

Then the rabbi had his turn to question the priest. He said, "Your religion too forbids certain things. I know you're supposed to be celibate ... but ...?"

The priest replied, "I know what you're going to ask. Yes, I have succumbed once or twice."

There was a silence for a while. Then the rabbi peered around the newspaper he was reading and said, "Better than pork, ain't it?"

♣

The IRA man killed in a bomb blast is met at the Pearly Gates by St. Peter.

"I'm O'Hara of the Belfast branch," says he.

"Well, you can't come in here," says St. Peter. "We don't want all that trouble in heaven."

"Oh, I don't want to come in," says O'Hara. "You've got ten minutes to clear the place."

Are you aware that the first man to set foot on the moon, Captain Neil Armstrong, had an Irish connection?

A reporter once recalled how impressed he was with his words as he stepped on the moon's surface. "That's one small step for man, and one giant step for mankind."

"How did you think of that?' asked the reporter "that was brilliant"

"Well actually," admitted Armstrong, " I didn't. It was written for me by NASA." And then he added, "but what I'd like to have said was, Go for it now, Mrs O'Reilly."

"Why would you say something like that?" inquired the reporter in astonishment.

"Well, said Armstrong "I grew up in an Irish neighbourhood and the O'Reillys lived next door and the walls between the apartments were very thin. Time and time again I'd hear Mrs O'Reilly say, "There'll be a man on the moon before I'll put that in me mouth."

So when I finally got to walk on the moon I wanted to say, "Go for it now, Mrs. O'Reilly, go for it now!"

During the cold war a top Russian KGB agent was given a difficult undercover mission. He was to travel deep through enemy territory, managing to stay only a step ahead of the CIA and MI6 who were hot on this trail. He was to meet with Murphy, the Irish spy, off the West Coast of Ireland, who would give him further directions.

The agent was told he would recognize Murphy by saying "The rain in Spain stays mainly in the plain," to which Murphy would reply," Mary had a little lamb, it's fleece was white as snow."

After several hectic weeks, the KGB agent eventually rows his small dinghy ashore into the harbour of a small Irish village. It is 5 a.m. and there is no one around except the milkman. He approaches him and asks:

"Is there a person by the name of Murphy here?"

"Oh yes, indeed," says the milkman. "Sure there's Murphy the school teacher, Murphy the policeman, Murphy the fireman, Murphy the doctor, Murphy the postman, Murphy the carpenter, and I'm Murphy the milkman."

At this the spy says, "The rain in Spain stays mainly in the plain," to which Murphy the milkman says,

"Ah, you'll be looking for Murphy the spy."

It was the end of the Gulf War and the Arabs stared over the oil fields and watched them burn. Day and night the flames roared into the sky and the Arabs pondered on how they were going to put out the fires, when one Arab suggested they ring "Red O'Dare."

Red O'Dare was contacted, but told the Arabs he was busy for the next six months. He suggested they contact his cousin Paddy O'Dare from County Mayo in Ireland.

The Arabs got on the phone and contacted Paddy. They explained their problem with the oil fields and asked if he could help. Paddy replied, "No problem."

The Arabs then asked him how quickly he could get there, and how much it would cost. Paddy replied, "I can be there in ten hours, and it'll cost ya' $10,000."

"Great," said the Arabs, and agreed to the terms. The Arabs waited in the desert, still watching the flames hoot into the sky when, all of a sudden, an open truck with four red-haired Paddys comes roaring over the sand dunes and heads straight into the oil field.

The Arabs shouted at them but to no avail, and the truck drove straight into one of the burning rigs. The riders jumped out, took off their denim jackets and proceeded to beat out the fire with them.

The Arabs watched in amazement, but two days later

the oil rig fire was out. The four Paddys walked to the
Arabs. One of them exclaimed, "Jazuz, that was rough!"
"It was," agreed the Arab, "but here's your check for
$10,000. What are you going to do with all this money?"

"Well, the first thing I am going to buy is a set of
brakes for that feckin' truck!"

♣

Paddy was visiting New York. He was patiently
waiting and watching the traffic cop on a busy street
crossing. The cop stopped the flow of traffic and
shouted, "Okay, pedestrians." Then he'd allow the
traffic to pass. He'd done this several times, yet Paddy
still stood on the sidewalk. After the cop had shouted
"Pedestrians" for the tenth time Paddy went over to
the cop and said, "Is it not about time ye let the
Catholics across?"

Irish Efficiency

Two sisters, Mary and Eileen, were rustic girls who lived in the region of Ballycastle, and worked in Ballymena, about twenty miles away.

For transportation they had a single bicycle between them. Mary would ride the bike for some minutes and then leave it at the roadside for Eileen, and continue on foot.

When Eileen reached the bike she would use it to cycle for a while and leave it for her sister. So it would go on.

The cycling time was set according to conditions, fair share and minimizing of bicycle idle time.

Talent Night

By Dave Abbott

I n 1943 the war in Europe was at its bloodiest and thousands of Irishmen, many with large families, were soldiering with the British Army.

Most of the families left behind had little money for food or clothing. Basic items like sugar, tea and flour were scarce and expensive, so families subsisted mainly on potatoes – boiled, sliced, diced, fried, chipped or baked.

The favoured recipe was "colcannon," which was boiled potatoes and boiled cabbage, mashed together and served with lots of salt and slathered in butter. By Irish standards it was considered a delicacy.

There were also occasional charitable evenings when the goodness of the church made it worthwhile being a parishioner. One such evening was the Annual Amateur Talent Contest.

The venue for this event was the 19th century granite hall adjoining St. Mary's Parish Church on the outskirts of Dublin. The inside of the parish hall was colder than an Englishman's handshake (it being mid-November), but saints be praised, there were two old-fashioned pot-bellied black stoves, fully stoked and radiating enough heat to warm the coldest heart.

An overflow crowd was expected for it was common knowledge that plates of fresh-baked sugar-coated buns, steaming rhubarb pie and piping hot sweet tea would be served after the contest.

"Aah sure 'n it'll be a grand feed," the Vicar's wife, Mrs. Grace O'Riordan would promise. "A feed not seen since pussy was a cat," I'd hear her say although I had no idea what she meant.

The contest attracted every amateur singer, musician, dancer and ham from the surrounding parishes and, for the most part, they were friendly with one another.

The lure of the prize money (seven and sixpence for first; five shillings for second; and half a crown for third) was secondary to winning the "bragging" rights represented by a perpetual trophy, a silver chalice, so badly stained the previous winner's names were indecipherable.

Winning was serious business and side bets were taken as to the likely outcome. Winning a talent contest was highly prized for a "fierce" talent reflected well on a family.

Naturally character assassination and pass-remarkable comments were an integral part of the evening. The craic and the slagging were choice and juicy.

48

"Sure, isn't that why we're here?" they'd say if asked.

"Did ye get a look at that one, mutton dressed up as lamb."

Or, "Jayzus, me cat sings better than that," or "Will ye look at her. Who does she think she is?"

"The fix is in, deffo, the fix is in. Those judges are just a load of bollocks."

The four judges were indeed cause for much derision since they were supposedly selected for their affinity and knowledge of the "Arts."

"Arts" was used in a catholic sense, for the panel included two wealthy spinsters, the Misses Patience and Penelope Crozier, who took up painting after, it was rumoured, dispatching their wealthy father prematurely to his grave to speed their inheritance.

"They poisoned his tea with boiled nettles," Mary Carmody, the maid, had pronounced with a finality that closed the matter. Rumour also had it they painted nudes of each other.

The third member of the jury was the Vicar, the Right Rev. Adrian Randolph Horatio O'Riordan. "A long drink of water with one good eye," as my mother described him, whose pet expression was a lisping "bweath my soul, bweath my soul."

Completing the four-person panel was the mortician-faced Fergus O'Toole, a scrawny, dark-suited man who had toiled for thirty years as a ticket taker at the Abbey Theatre. His face was fixed in a permanent sneer, a legacy from a childhood bout with polio and, according to parish gossip, he affected airs and graces "far above his station in life." Patty Pope always took pains to point out that "tearing ticket stubs in half hardly qualifies as 'Art.'"

Our contestants were a diverse group. John Costello was a seventy-something pasty-faced Irish tenor who wore a green bow tie and sang a quartertone flat. There was a seventy-something soprano, Nellie Cronhelm, who wobbled, quivered and quavered, with a turkey gullet, sounding like a stuck gramophone needle, coming close – only close – to high C.

Following her were the twins, Jessie and Gertie Stumph, two eleven-year-old pear-shaped daughters of the local butcher with pigtails and floor-length frocks which made them look like pup tents at a Bavarian beer festival.

The banjo player was a retired housepainter from Cork who called himself Ireland's George Formby and sang "When I'm Cleaning Windows," in an unintelligible Yorkshire Geordie accent and thick Irish brogue.

A Shirley Temple look-alike, a six-year-old student of

ballet, Ruth Miriam Isobel Kilbey, sat in the front row nervously chewing her lip and kicking the legs of her chair while waiting her turn.

Arthur Maloney preceded me. A solemn man with a face like a battered hat, wearing horn-rimmed spectacles, who beat time with the steel taps on his shoes, and banged cymbals strapped to his knees for the syncopated rhythm, while giving a rendition of "Paddy McGinty's Goat," with a comb and tissue paper.

And then it was my turn – the ubiquitous boy soprano. Dressed in a brown velvet suit, which my mother had made, complete with a white shirt and tartan bow tie, I was hot and nervous climbing up the steps to the stage to sing "Christopher Robin Is Saying His Prayers."

Kneeling downstage I lit the candle, placing it in a brass holder. The lights were doused and folding my hands in prayer I began singing, "Christopher Robin Is Saying His Prayers." When I came to the part, "hush, hush, don't you cry," a draft from an opened door blew out the candle, leaving me in total darkness.

I stopped, started again, finally completing the song in embarrassment and rushed offstage, falling headfirst down the steps into the waiting balletomane, the young Miss Kilbey. She crashed to the floor with her knickers showing

51

and me on top in the missionary position. Both of us were unharmed, but I was mortified as I heard a loudly whispered, "Jayzus, what 'n eejit."

I finished out of the prize money but I married the ballerina.

The Craic

The Gaelic word "craic" (pronounced "crack") refers to the ability to give a quick retort, a verbal thrust, a sharp riposte while engaged in conversation. It is also known as a form of "slagging" whereby a person is humiliated by words or put in their place verbally. The more clever the reply, the more the person is respected and admired. Dubliners are known for their love of "craic."

Hey," said a new arrival in the pub, "I've got some great Irish jokes."

"Before you start," said the big bloke in the corner, "I'm warning you, I'm Irish."

"Don't worry," said the newcomer, "I'll tell them slowly."

♣

Paddy and Mick win the lottery and share first prize of $2 million. They're celebrating their winnings over a pint. "But Paddy, I've been thinking," said Mick with a worried frown, "what will we do with all them beggin' letters?"

"Sure," said Paddy, "we'll go on sending 'em out."

The origin of the bagpipes was being discussed and the representatives of different nations were eagerly disclaiming responsibility for the instrument. Finally an Irishman said, "Well, I'll tell you the truth about it. The Irish invented them and sold them to the Scots as a joke and the Scots haven't seen the joke yet."

♣

The Aer Lingus plane was in serious trouble. "Mayday, Mayday," radioed the pilot.
"Cleared to land," came the answer from the control tower. "Can you give us your height and position?"
"Well," said the pilot, " I'm five eight and I'm sittin' at the front of the plane."

♣

An airman had to bail out of a failing airplane, but landed battered and bruised in a field just outside of Belfast. A crowd had gathered round, and one of them asked the airman, "What happened?"
He said, "My parachute wouldn't open."
The Irishman said, "Ye should have known. Nuttin' opens here on a Sunday."

Did you hear about the Irish newlyweds who sat up all night on their honeymoon waiting for their sexual relations to arrive?

♣

Two Irishmen are sitting on an iceberg. Paddy says to Murphy, "We're going to be saved, we're going to be saved."

Murphy asked, "How do ye know that?"

Paddy replies, "Here comes the *Titanic*."

♣

"Don't jump," yelled Paddy to the man on the ledge.

"Think of your wife and children."

"I've got not wife or children."

"Then think of your parents."

"I don't have any parents."

"Then think of St. Patrick."

"Who's St. Patrick?"

"Jump, ya bastard!"

Paddy was an inveterate drunkard. The priest met him one day, and gave him a very stern lecture about the evils of drink. He warned him; "If you continue drinking as you do, you'll gradually get smaller and smaller, and eventually you'll turn into a mouse."

This frightened the life out of Paddy. He went home that night and said to his wife, "Bridget, if you should notice me getting smaller and smaller, will ye kill that blasted cat?"

♣

An Englishman walks into a country pub in the county of Galway. "I say," he says. "How very quaint! All of this sawdust on the floor."

"Ah," replies the barman, "that's not sawdust. That's last night's furniture."

♣

The Irishman at the front door said, "Morning, missus. I've come to mend your doorbell."

"I was expecting you yesterday," the woman replied.

"Sure now, but I rang then and got no answer."

And then there was the Irish gardener who broke his collarbone while raking up leaves – he fell out of the tree.

♣

An American tourist was visiting the Ulster Museum in Belfast and asked the age of a particular fossil.

The attendant told him it was three million years and nine months old.

"How on earth can they be so accurate?" asked the visitor.

The attendant replied, "Well, sir, when I started work here they me it was three million years old, and I'm here nine months."

♣

Driving in Ireland means dealing with flocks of sheep, herds of cattle and clutches of ducks and geese, all of which frequent the roads of Ireland. Some are being driven to or from the market. Some are being driven to or from the pastures. Others are there, in my view, because there is a sporting chance they'll get hit by a car and return a quick profit to the owner.

But not all Irishmen are dumb. After all it was an Irishman who invented the helicopter ejection seat. And did you know it was an Irish surgeon who developed the appendix transplant, and an Irishman who invented a solar-powered flashlight?

♣

A Dublin newspaper office recently received an unusual call.

"We have seen," said the feminine voice, "a number of references in the press to the law of supply and demand.

Could you kindly inform us what this law is, and when it was passed?"

♣

A woman telephoned an airline office in Dublin and asked, "How long does it take to fly to London?"

The clerk said "Just a minute."

"Thank you" said the woman and hung up.

♣

That same Irish woman's nephew was the one who moved his house two feet forward – to take up the slack in his clothesline.

58

"Sean," said Mick, "did you know we only use one third of our brains?"

"No!" said Sean. "What happens to the other third?"

♣

Then there was Murphy, who upon being told he had two weeks to live decided to take a week in July and the other in September.

♣

An Irish lawyer, having the occasion to go to dinner, left these directions written and put them in the keyhole of his chamber door:

"I am gone to the *O'Dwyer's* where you shall find me. If you can't read this note, carry it next door and my neighbour will read it for you."

♣

The Irish attempt on Mount Everest was a valiant effort, but it failed; they ran out of scaffolding.

♣

Kelly had two horses, and he could never tell them apart. It caused him lots of trouble until one day he discovered that the black horse was two hands taller than the white one.

Paddy was trapped in a bog and seemed a goner when Big Mick O'Reilly walked by.

"Help," Paddy shouted, " I'm sinking."

"Don't worry," assured Mick, I'm the strongest man in Ireland -- I'll pull you out."

Mick leaned over and grabbed Paddy's hand and pulled and pulled and pulled, but to no avail. After two more unsuccessful attempts Mick said to Paddy,

"I'm the strongest man in Ireland, if I can't pull you out I'll have to get some help."

Just as Mick was about to leave Paddy shouted,

"Mick, Mick, do you think if will help if I take my feet out of the stirrups?"

♣

Murphy was selling his house and put the matter in a real estate agent's hands. The agent wrote his advertisement for the house and made it wonderful reading.

After Murphy read it, he turned to the gent and asked,

"Have I got all ye say there?"

The agent said, "Certainly ye have . . . Why?"

Murphy replied, "Cancel the sale, 'tis too good to part with."

Paddy's brother was visiting America and while there went into a pizza parlour. When his pizza was ready the man behind the counter asked Paddy whether he wanted it cut into four or into six pieces.

"Better make it four," said Paddy's brother. " I don't think I could eat six."

♣

A famous writer visiting Ireland asked an Irish colleague whether there was any word in the Irish language that had the same meaning as the Spanish manana. The Irishman pondered well before replying. "Sure," he said, "we've about two or three that come close. But none of 'em have the same sense of urgency."

♣

An English gent was coming home late one night when a masked man popped out of an alley and said, "This is a hold up. Put your hands up, or else!"

"Or else what?" asked the gent testily.

"Don't be gettin' me confused," the masked man said, hoarsely, "This is me first job."

An Irishman was held up by a bandit with the usual demand:

"Your money or your life!"

"Take my life," said the Irishman. " I'll be after saving me money for me old age."

♣

An Irishman was being held up in a dark street in Belfast.

"Catholic or Protestant?" demanded the thief in a threatening tone.

Thinking quickly to save his skin, Seamus replied

"Actually, I'm Jewish."

"Well," replied the robber with a leer, "aren't I just the luckiest Arab in Belfast tonight?"

♣

An Irish delinquent was in court for non-payment of maintenance to his previous wife. The magistrate weighed the case and said "I've decided to increase this allowance, and give your wife five pounds per week.

Pat said, "Ye're a gentleman Sir. I might send her a few bob meself too."

Mick decided to join police force and went along for the entrance examination. The examining sergeant, realising that the prospective recruit was an Irishman, decided to ask him a simple question. "Who killed Jesus Christ?" he asked.

Mick looked worried and said nothing, so the sergeant told him not to worry and that he could have some time to think about it.

Mick was on his way home when he met Paddy.

"Well," said Paddy, "are you a policeman yet?"

"Not only that," says Mick proudly, "but I'm already on my first case."

♣

The Birmingham landlady wanted to please her Irish lodger and the first day she gave him two slices of bread for his package lunch. He didn't seem satisfied, so she gave him four slices the next day, and then six slices had to go on, until he was getting ten.

Even this wasn't enough so, in desperation, she cut the loaf in half and put ham between the pieces. When he came in that evening she asked, "Had you enough today, Colum?"

"It wasn't bad," he said grudgingly, "but I see you're back to the two slices again.

Bridget, the maid, picked up the phone and muttered something before slamming it down.

"Who was that, Bridget?" I'm expecting a trunk call."

"Only some mad idiot, Mr. Slattery. He said it was a long distance from California. I told him we knew."

♣

Bryant caught a tiny fish, which suddenly began to speak. "I'm really an elf and if you release me I'll grant you and your wife any three wishes."

So the Irishman released the fish, rushed home and told his wife. The couple was anxious to get to town and look at things to wish for, so the wife decided to make a quick dinner out of a can of beans. But she couldn't find the can opener and said, "I wish I had a can opener." *Kazam!* She had a can opener.

"You wasted one wish on that stupid can opener," screamed Bryant. "I wish it was up your ass."

And the sad part of the story is that they had to use the third and last wish to get it out again.

♣

Then there was the old lady who thought her horse was certain to win the Irish Derby because the bookie told her it would start at twenty-to-one and the race didn't begin until a quarter past.

64

The phone rang in the hospital in Galway. The nurse lifted the phone and a voice said, "I'm enquiring about Pat Murphy, who had a very serious operation last week. I can't sleep worrying about him. Can you find out how the operation went?

Is he going to be all right, and when might he be going home?"

The nurse said, "Hold on."

She went away and came back about ten minutes later and said, "Well, I talked to the doctor and he said the operation went well, and he's back in his bed. If he continues to make progress he could be going home in about two weeks. May I ask who's calling?"

"Pat Murphy," came the reply. "Nobody tells me anything around here."

♣

Seamus O'Brien had been hailed the most intelligent Irish man for three years running. He had topped such shows as the "Just A Minute Quiz" and "Quicksilver." The Irish Mensa Board suggested he should enter the English Mastermind Championships. On the evening of the competition, Seamus entered from the crowd and placed himself on the contestant's seat and made himself comfortable. The lights dimmed and a spotlight shone on him.

The master of ceremonies, asked Seamus, "What subject are you studying?" Seamus responded, "Irish history."

"Very well," the MC responded, "here's your first question."

"In what year did the Easter Rising take place?"

"Pass," Seamus responded.

"All right, then," Magnus continued. "Who was the leader of the Easter Rising?"

"Pass," Seamus said.

"OK," Magnus continued. "How long did the Easter Rising last?"

Seamus responded once more, "Pass."

At this point a voice shouted out from the crowd in the theatre, "Good man, Seamus.

Tell the English nothing."

♣

Pat and Mick met after not seeing each other for a long time.

"Whatcha doin' now, Mick?" Pat asked his friend.

"I'm studying at University College in Dublin."

"Jazuz," replied Pat, "and what are ye studyin'?"

"Logic," replied Mick.

"What's logic?" asked Pat.

"Well," said Mick, "it's like this. D'ye have a goldfish?"

"I do," says Pat.

"So, you probably have the fish for your kids."

"That's right," Pat replies.

"So, having kids means you're probably married."

"That's right again," says Pat.

"So being married means you're not a homosexual," Mick continued.

"That's right," Pat says in amazement.

"It's logic that allows me to figure this out," said Mick

They said their goodbyes, and shortly thereafter Pat met his friend Seamus.

"Hey, Seamus," Pat says, "I just met Mick, and he's studying logic at the University College."

"What's logic?" Seamus asked.

"Let me explain," said Pat. "Do you have goldfish?"

"Yes," said Seamus.

"Then you're not a homosexual!"

The Boston taxi driver backed into the stationary fruit stall and in a second he had a Copper beside him.

"Name?"

"Brendan O'Connor."

"Same as mine," said the cop. "Where you from?"

"Co. Leitrim."

"Same as me . . .. "

The policeman paused with his pen in the air.

"Hold on a moment and I'll come back and talk about the old country. I want to say something to this fellow that ran into the back of your cab."

♣

Two cannibals were talking and one complained that he got an awful pain after eating an Irish Franciscan missionary.

"How did you cook him?" asked the chief.

"I boiled him."

"That explains it," nodded the chief sagely. "You should never boil Franciscans. They're Friars."

One fine sunny morning the priest took a walk in the local forest. Walking by a small stream when he noticed a very sad looking frog sitting on a toadstool.

"What's wrong with you?" said the priest.

"Well," said the frog, "the reason I am so sad on this fine day is because I wasn't always a frog."

"Really!" said the priest. "Can you explain?"

"Once upon a time I was an 11-year-old choir boy at the local church. I too was walking through this forest when I was confronted by a wicked witch. "Let me pass," I yelled, but to no avail. She called me a cheeky little boy, and with a flash of her wand, turned me into a frog."

"That's an incredible story," said the priest. "Is there no way of reversing the spell the witch cast on you?"

"Well, yes," said the frog. "It is said that if a nice, kind person would pick me up, take me home and give me food and warmth and with a good night's sleep, would wake up the boy once again."

"Today's your lucky day," said the priest, and picked up the frog and took him home. The priest gave the frog lots of food, placed him by the fire and at bedtime put the frog on the pillow beside him. When the priest awoke, he saw the 11-year-old choirboy beside him in bed.

"And that, my lord is the case for the Defense . . ."

O'Brien asked his wife what she wanted for her birthday. She said, "I'd like something with diamonds in it." O'Brien bought her a pack of cards.

♣

Casey was in court and pleads not guilty to the charge. Later he changed his plea to guilty. The judge asked him "Why did you change your mind." Casey replied, "Well, your honour, I thought I was innocent 'til I heard the evidence against me."

♣

Murphy: "This clock will run for 30 days without winding."

Casey: "Great. How long will it run if you wind it?"

♣

Flanagan approached a beautiful young lady at a very dull party and said, "Would you please talk to me for a few minutes. I want to go home and watch a football match on television and if my wife sees me talking to you she'll say 'It's time to go home.'"

Quotables

There are many memorable quotes from the pens of the writers, poets and politicians of Ireland. The dry wit, the quick response, the right word for the right occasion have been grist for the mill for centuries. Here are just a few:

Smiles cost nothing, yet they are most valuable, particularly when exchanged.

♣

Irish diplomacy: The ability to tell a man to go to hell in such a way that he'll look forward to making the trip.

♣

The Irish lover was heard to say, "It's a great comfort to be alone, especially when yer sweetheart is with ye."

♣

Some men have half a mind to go into politics – that is all you need nowadays.

♣

The only people who listen to both sides of an argument are the neighbours.

♣

Irish definition of a grandparent: something so simple even a child can operate it.

Only Irish coffee provides in a single glass all four essential food groups: alcohol, caffeine, sugar and fat.

Alex Levine

♣

Maybe it's bred in the bone, but the sound of pipes is a little bit of heaven to some of us. *Nancy O'Keefe*

♣

Good resolutions are merely cheques that men draw on a bank where they have no account.

♣

Both your friend and your enemy think you will never die.

♣

Good as drink is, it ends in thirst.

The Behans

Undoubtedly the most famous member of the Behan family was Brendan. His brother, Dominic, was also a talented writer, but never enjoyed the success of his brother.

Brendan Behan

By Dave Abbott

One of the salubrious spots where Dublin's literati meet was Davey Byrnes' lounge bar on Duke Street.

In the fifties it was here that, for the price of a pint, one could listen to the likes of Brendan Behan or Paddy Kavanagh, riveting each other with verbal guns, their tongues slicing and cutting each other with the famed Dublin *'craic'*.

The 'craic' is a gift, a blessing, ranking higher than an undergraduate degree and like 'slagging' its pedigree dates back millennia in the oral tradition of the Irish.

The highest accolade was reserved for the articulate verbal gymnast and slagger Oscar Wilde, whom George Bernard Shaw pronounced as "the greatest talker of his time, perhaps of all time." Obviously Shaw hadn't met Brendan Behan who arrived some years later.

A better playwright than novelist, this once-upon-a-time Borstal-boy- would-be IRA terrorist, held court 'performing' in pubs around the city.

Suffering from infuriating and incessant mood changes, which generally occurred in direct proportion to his alcoholic intake, he possessed all the true appendages of a clown with a multifunctional face suitable for vaudeville. Loquacious, eccentric, verbally violent and completely egocentric he specialised in shock and startle tactics, like the soldier of fortune he claimed to be. He had been jailed for his perverse beliefs in the 'ould cause' of mother Ireland.

As students we'd sip our solitary pints eavesdropping on this rollicking bollicking oratorical genius with his 'big feckin put-on' revealing his phobias, loves, hates and woes in a spectacle of alcohol-induced fiery rhetoric and lewdness. He had a fine singing voice and a superb repertoire to accompany his feckless stories.

I recall returning to Dublin from London, after attending Joan Littlewood's staging of *The Quare Fellow,* and running into Brendan on Grafton Street. "Hey Brendan," I shouted enthusiastically, "I just saw your play in London and it was feckin' great."

I had hoped to engage him in conversation but instead he unleashed a deafening roar. " Ah jayzus, another paying feckin' customer" he shouted and staggered drunkenly into Davey Byrnes Lounge for more sustenance.

To many middle-class Dubliners he was little more than a bowser, a gurrier, notwithstanding his literary achievements, which were gifts clearly bestowed by God in error. Dubliners always criticized their own and were 'begrudgers' of fellow countrymen who achieved a measure of success. As George Bernard Shaw said, "The Irish are a fair race. They always speak ill of each other."

A close friend of Brendan, Peter Arthurs, wrote, "He saw himself as a rogue, a rascal, a brilliant talker, a roaring conundrum; a supple-fleshed pugnacious brawler who was both world-loved and despised."

Many years later Brendan appeared on a CBC television talk show, six sheets to the wind, looking like he hadn't slept in a week. He proceeded to tell the world that Vancouver "is a terrible hole; Canada is barbaric without being picturesque; and Toronto will be a fine town when it's finished."

Unshaven, purple faced, his hair matted, he could hardly sit still in the chair during the interview. He died a few months later of booze and diabetes. He was 42.

"Too young to die, too drunk to live" read one Behan obituary.

Let's Celebrate!

B rendan Behan once told the story of how he got a job in London with a street repair gang. The first job he went to they were down in a hole singing Happy Birthday around the foreman. "Is it the foreman's birthday?" asked Brendan.

"No, Brendan. It's the third anniversary of the hole."

♣

One night Behan collapsed in a diabetic coma in a Dublin street. It was at a time when he was at the height of his drunken notoriety and passers-by naturally thought he was dead drunk. They took him to the nearby surgery of one of Dublin's most fashionable and respected doctors. The doctor decided to take a cardiograph and, somewhat nervous of his patient, thought to humour him. He explained the workings of the cardiograph needle as it registered the faint heartbeats of the very sick and semi-conscious Brendan.

"That needle there is writing down your pulses, Mr. Behan, and I suppose, in its own way, it is probably the most important thing you have ever written."

To which Behan replied, "Aye, and it's straight from me heart, too."

Kathleen Behan

Despite being a real "Dub" Kathleen Behan was loved throughout Ireland. She wined and dined with the best but never forgot her roots. Her company was much sought after.

Auld Dublin Stock

By Dave Abbott

B rendan Behan's mother, Kathleen, was an extraordinary woman with a prodigious memory for stories and songs.

She was a neighbour of the redoubtable Mrs. Brown, mother of *"My Left Foot"* Christy Brown, who had given birth to twenty-two children. Kathleen had given birth to eleven children of which only six had survived. Some were stillborn, others died in infancy.

Yet both these remarkable women had each contributed a son to the Irish literary scene, Christy and Brendan, both of whom died at an early age.

Kathleen had been a long time widow when we met through a mutual friend, Ulick O'Connor. She had outlived her husband Steven (Joe), a housepainter by trade and well-known around Dublin for driving a funeral hearse for his decorating business. He was known to have been fond of the drink.

As soon as I landed in Dublin, I'd call Kathleeen and arrange to pay her a visit. I usually came in the early afternoon by taxi, collecting her from her typical Dublin County Council house.

In latter years I had to travel to the outer suburbs to collect her at the Sisters of Charity, a seniors rest home, where the nuns took good care of her. They treated her kindly but remained firmly committed to their policy of no smoking or drinking. But Kathleen missed her 'gargle.'

Always impeccably dressed, Kathleen would greet me in a black coat over a modest high-necked white blouse and ankle length grey skirt topped with a small black flowered hat perched jauntily askew on her tiny frame.

The taxi driver upon seeing her would spring out of his seat to open the door.

"Hello, Mrs. Behan. Nice to see you. Howa yeh?" he'd say with ostentatiousness and formality, like he was greeting Her Majesty the Queen.

"I'm grand," she'd say "just grand."

She was everyone's long-suffering mother, and like all Irish mothers, a martyr to her sons.

'Sweet jayzus', they'd say, "wasn't Brendan a terrible cross to bear?"

She'd settle herself in the back seat, and leaning over

she'd whisper, "Did you bring a drop of the ould crater for me David?" At which point I'd produce the bottle of Paddy whiskey and receive a smiling "Aah David, you're a grand man, a grand man," and giving a little sigh of contentment she'd straighten her hat as she gazed lovingly out the window at her darlin' dirty Dublin passing by.

I usually took her directly to the Shelbourne Hotel, where her arrival always caused a flurry of attention and caused more of a flap than any visiting head of state or movie star.

The doorman tipped his hat, the concierge and bellhops chorused "Hello Mrs. Behan" as the waiters rushed to serve us. I basked in the glow of her celebrity for, as a friend of Kathleen Behan, my 'stock' increased appreciably amongst the hotel personnel and other guests.

Once in the room she'd take off her coat, plunk herself down, fold her legs demurely and regale me with stories and songs from Ireland's past.

Over the next few hours she'd demolish the bottle of whiskey, 'holy water' as she called it, preferring it straight for she didn't want to 'spoil it' with ice or mixer, and then she'd start singing in a clear voice:

In Dublin's fair city, where girls are so pretty,
I first set my eyes on sweet Molly Malone
As she wheeled her wheelbarrow
Thru streets broad and narrow
Cryin' "Cockles and mussels, alive, alive, o!"
Alive, alive oh o!
Alive, alive oh o!
Cryin' "Cockles and mussels, alive, alive o"
She was a fishmonger but sure 'twas no wonder,
For so were her father and mother before;
And they both wheeled their barrow
Thru streets broad and narrow
Cryin' "Cockles and mussels alive, alive o!"
Alive, alive oh o!
Alive, alive oh o!
Cryin' "Cockles and mussels, alive, alive o!"
She died of a fever and no one could save her
And that was the end of sweet Molly Malone,
But her ghost wheels her barrow
Thru streets broad and narrow
Cryin' "Cockles and mussels, alive, alive o!"

Throughout the course of the afternoon flowers, fruit, tea and ham sandwiches would arrive, courtesy of the Hotel manager but they were of no interest to Kathleen.

"Could I have a few stout," she'd ask, "to wash the food down?"

"Ah you're a grand man, a Dublin jewel."

She'd cackle charmingly, relishing the pint, the Guinness trademark white moustache on her lively elfin face, but leaving the tea untouched.

She was filled with surprises.

"Did ye know me brother Peadar Carney wrote the National Anthem?" she'd ask, "Did ye ever know Biddy Mulligan the pride of the Coombe?" her eyes twinkling and without botherin' for an answer she'd launch into song.

"And that old triangle
Went jingle jangle
All along the banks of the Royal Canal"

It was a refrain she taught Brendan on her knee, and continued to sing long after her son had died.

Returning Katherine to the nuns at the rest home was often an embarrassment for she was always 'stocious' but the Sisters of Charity knew how to handle her.

She claimed they made her pray three times daily for a whole month in the convent chapel as an act of contrition. I never knew whether to believe her or not.

Holy Water

One of the most popular tourist stops in Dublin is a tour of the famous Guinness brewery, renowned world-wide for its black stout, which at one time employed more than half of Dublin's work force. And that industry was the result of many an old Irish favourite, such as this one:

Two oul wans, Mrs. O'Reilly and Mrs. O'Toole meet on the street. Both their husbands worked at Guinness's, so they knew one another.

"Oh, Mrs. O'Toole, I was so sorry to hear that himself drowned in a vat of Guinness last week. We were all overcome with the horror of it all. What a dreadful way to go – drowning in a vat of Guinness. It must have been a very painful death."

"Ah," says Mrs. O'Toole, "it's very sad, very tragic. But it really wasn't such a dreadful way to go. Not atall, atall."

"Not painful?" cried Mrs. O'Reilly, "drowning in a vat of Guinness?"

"Ahh, no," says Mrs. O'Toole. "Sure didn't he climb out three times for a piss."

Quick Recipe for Irish Stew

We've got our own recipe for Irish stew.

Get some meat, some potatoes and a lot of Guinness stout. Drink all of the stout. Forget about the stew.

♣

Dean Jonathan Swift, author of *Gulliver's Travels*, once said, "Drink is the curse of this country. It makes you quarrel with your landlord. It makes you shoot at your landlord – and it makes you MISS him!"

♣

Do you know what's written on the bottom of an Irish whiskey bottle?

"Open other end."

What's written on the top of an Irish whiskey bottle?

"See other end for instructions."

Limericks

Limericks are clever plays on words — a favourite Irish pastime. It is thought this form of verse originated in the county of Limerick, home to actor Richard Harris and author Frank McCourt.

Do you think if I poured you some gin again,"
Asked Finnegan, "You might care to sin again?"
Said she with a grin,
"You want it back in,
You must pay me a fin again — Finnegan!"

♣

There was a young colleen named Flynn
Who thought fornication a sin,
But when she was tight,
It seemed quite all right;
So everyone filled her with gin.

♣

A colleen of fair Ballycrotty,
Loved men of all colours — 'twas dotty,
But her children are a sight,
Every heart to delight,
For they're black, brown, green-striped and half spotty.

A great Irish thinker named Berkely,
Expressed his belief, oh, so starkly.
    "Almost all that we see,
    Cannot possibly be,
And the rest I conceive is unlarkly."

♣

A western young lady named Flynn,
Would tell of her plans with a grin,
    "I intend to be bold,
    In manner untold,
For there's need of original sin."

♣

A ghost in the town of Macroom
One night found a ghoul in his room.
    They argued all night,
    As to which had the right,
To frighten the wits out of whom.

'Tis famous, the food of Killarney,
As tasty and fresh as sweet Blarney.
     Knowing well it is nice
     When served fast on ice,
Gourmets shriek for the Chilly Con Kearney.

♣

The puritan people of Teeling,
Express all their horrors with feeling.
     When they see that a chair,
     Has all its legs bare,
They look away straight to the ceiling.

♣

There was an old man of Tralee,
Who was bothered a bit by a flea,
     So he put out the light,
     Saying, "Now he can't bite,
For he'll never be able to see."

A nun in a convent in Bray,
Saw her roses go into decay,
  Reverend Mother, said "Dear,
  Please no longer fear,
It's liquid manure, let us spray."

♣

A happy young colleen from Derry,
On ale was loving and merry,
  She dallied with sin,
  On vodka and gin,
But was rigid and frigid on sherry.

♣

The fairy banshee moans and moans,
For she's known for her musical groans,
  She wails in B sharp,
  Like a dyspeptic harp,
Winning prizes for anguished octones.

A "lady" they called her in Trim,
Though her right to the title was slim.
 And doubts started to mount,
 With her chromosome count,
Was she "her" or an "it" or a "him?"

♣

A neurotic in old Ballindine,
Lay down on a railway line,
 But it was such a bore,
 For the four-forty-four,
Didn't come 'til a quarter past nine.

♣

A coy maiden of Glenmalure,
Had a mind that was perfectly pure.
 She fainted away
 In a delicate way,
If anyone spoke of manure.

A girl from Belfast name of Alice,
Drew rude things on the Vatican Palace.
>   She said, "Now this deed
>   Comes from aesthetic need,
And not from a Protestant malice."

♣

The widow of Ballinalickey,
Was married eight times and was tricky.
>   She led without falter
>   Young Mike to the altar,
They sang "Him" Number Nine for poor Mickey.

♣

A horse-loving lady of Howth,
Said, "I'm changing my diet to take nowth,
>   I intend for a start,
>   Not to dine à la carte,
But to eat with my table d'oat."

Signs

When translating Gaelic into English some "expressions" improve, others provide the ludicrous.

♣

Road sign near Killarney:
This is the wrong road to Dublin. Do not take this road.

♣

Sign seen in a home laundry:
Why kill yourself with washing? Let us do it by hand.

♣

Notice in a beauty shop:
Ears pierced while you wait.
Pay for two and get one done free.

♣

Notice on a shop:
Yes. We are open. Please call back at some other time.

♣

Newspaper headline:
Body of man found in graveyard!

The Sligo Spy

By Dave Abbott

One summer, flush with money after working as a bus conductor on the green double-decker buses on the Isle of Wight, I splurged on the latest in wireless technology — a Phillips portable radio to take back with me to Ireland.

It was a graduation present to myself to keep me company while living in the isolated West Coast farming town of Sligo as a resident professor at the local College. Irish country towns could be deadly dull.

It was a grand machine with a brown leather case and a top which flipped open to display a row of tuning buttons for long, medium and short-wave bands, plus the usual on/off knobs. The snazzy leather strap sat on my shoulder allowing it to hang by my side as I walked.

Radio was magic: a comforting companion, a pal and a link to the outside world. Invisible to the eye, it travelled on the wind, beamed from Europe on wavelengths like Radio Luxembourg, filling nights as black as a pint of Guinness, muffling the desolate sounds of the Atlantic's winds and icy rains with mellow voices and music.

The morning after my arrival, I strolled into town

buy fresh batteries for my spiffy portable wireless set.

Curious eyes, peeking through lace curtains, followed me down the road. In Irish country towns like Sligo the face of a stranger was cause for curiosity and comment.

The only shop selling batteries was Larkin's, the Chemist, who himself (now that I think about it) eyed me furtively as I undid the leather casing and extracted the eight large batteries from the base of the radio.

"Have you any like this?" I inquired with a smile.

"I tink I've got some 'o dem," he said, "but I've never seen a contraption like dat before. What d'ye call dat?" he asked suspiciously.

"A Phillips portable radio," I answered proudly.

"A radio? You don't say. A radio. Isn't that grand," he said stepping back a pace to view it with fresh eyes.

"Glory be, what will they think of next," he proclaimed like a Marconi discoverer.

"And does it work?" he asked.

"Oh yes, yes," I said, nodding my head, "but only after I put in these batteries. Let's find out," I said and switched it on. A few squeeks, buzzes and beeps emitting a high-pitched whine was all that emerged as I frantically twirled the buttons trying for a recognizable sound. Deep hums and the occasional shriek filled the shop. I had the volume

92

cranked right up, and a few curious shoppers gathered around, gawking. I tried again to tune in to something, but to no avail. Radio signals weren't meant to penetrate walls built in the 19th century.

After handing me my change, Mr. Larkin looked me up skeptically. "I'd ask for my money back is I was you. Are 'oo sure that's a real wireless now?"

Embarrassed, I left, quietly cursing under my breath; my prized possession had made me look foolish.

Outside the shop I twisted the knob to "on." Immediately splendid sounds, snatches of music, garbled languages, ships calling to each other; Morse code and lots of static spilled forth. Sounds from the "great Universe beyond" spoke to me. The tranquil village was transformed -- filled with a cacophony of voices and noises from afar.

Feeling very pleased with myself, I cautiously tuned in a German radio station playing a military march and happily jackbooted it back to the college, keeping time with the beat. I felt vindicated after Larkin's "are you sure it's a radio, now?"

That evening a small boy knocked on my bedroom door. "Please, sir, the Headmaster wants to see ye in his study."

The Headmaster, Richard "Dicky" Blackburn was a

bear of a man. Well over six feet tall with the smell of farmyard manure about him, and a personality that seemed more suited to nurturing heifers than children. He clearly loved his "calling" as he referred to it. He spoke with a soft brogue.

"Ah, Mr. Abbot. Have 'oo bin in Sligo town dis afturnoon?"

"Yes, Headmaster," I replied, thinking what a strange question it was.

"Was everyting all right? No problems were dere?" He smiled at me kindly.

Dickey Blackburn had an enormous bald head, with a shiny pate and his cheeks flowed into his jowls, giving him a perpetually sad hangdog look, reminding me of our basset hound back at home, Oliver St. John Gogarty.

"Ah, no, Headmaster. There were no problems," I said looking at him quizzically.

"Can I ask ye, where did ye go?"

He sounded exasperated.

"Go, Headmaster? Go? I went to Larkins, the Post Office, Wood's Hardware and then I returned to the college. That's all," I answered with a shrug.

"What's this all about then, Headmaster?" I asked politely.

94

He fixed his eyes on me like a setter pointing at a
shoot. "Ah got a couple of phone calls from friends of
mine who, aah, saw 'oo in town today, and they do tell me
'oo had some kind of machine wit ye."

"A machine, Headmaster?"

"Some sorta receiver ting makin' strange sounds, like
the Morse code an' foreign languages. Dat sorta ting. Some
thought ye might be one of dem spy fellas. They couldn't
make head nor tail of it," he finished lamely. His busy
eyebrows arched into question marks.

"A spy, Headmaster? Me? A Spy?"

I was about to laugh until I caught his eye. He was
serious — very serious. Then the penny dropped.

I excused myself. I'd be back in a minute or two to
explain.

I fetched the portable Phillips, and within minutes he
was playing with it. He was in awe of my "receiver ting"
and seemed satisfied with my "explanation."

But from that day on he never fully trusted me.

There remained in him a lingering suspicion that I
might be up to no good. "Spyin' and that sorta thing."

An Irishman's Philosophy

There are only two things to worry about:
>   Either you are well or you are sick.
If you are well, then there is nothing to worryabout.

But if you are sick, there are two things to worry about:
>   Either you will get well or you will die.
If you get well, then there is nothing to worry about.

But if you die, there are two things to worry about:
>   Either you will go to heaven or you will go to hell.
If you go to heaven, then you have nothing to worry about.

But if you go to hell, you'll be so damn busy shaking hands with all your friends that you won't have time to worry!

Cumallyis

The Irish speak with a lilt. Some call it a brogue, which is musical and transposes into song quite easily. Hence singing songs which told stories and provided all the news, especially in rural Ireland, were common. Some of them contained hundreds of verses and took hours to complete. Dublin "jackeens" called such songs "Cumallyis," as in "Come all of you and listen to my story."

From Derry quay we sailed away
   On the twenty-third of May
We were taken on board by a pleasant crew
Bound for Amerikay
Fresh water there we did take on
Five thousand gallons or more
In case we'd run short going to New York
Far away from the shamrock shore.
So fair the well, sweet Lisa dear
And likewise to Derry town
And twice farewell to my comrades bold
Who still dwell on that sainted ground
If ever kind fortunes does favour me
And I do have money in store
I'll come back and I'll wed that sweet girl I left
On Paddy's green shamrock shore.
We sailed three days and were all sea-sick

Not one on board was free
We were all confined unto our bunks
With no one to pity me
No fond mother dear or father kind
To comfort my head when 'twas sore
It made me think more of that sweet girl I left
On Paddy's green shamrock shore.
We safely reached the other side
In fifteen and twenty days
We were taken as passengers by a man
Who led us in six different ways
So then we all drank a parting glass
In case we would never meet more
And we drank a health to old Ireland dear
And to Paddy's green shamrock shore.
Oh, there's a brandy in Quebec at nine cents a quart, boys
The ale in New Brunswick is a penny a glass
And there's wine in that sweet town they call Montreal, boys
At inn after inn we shall drink as we pass.
And we'll call for a bumper of ale, wine and brandy
And we'll drink to the health of those far away
And our hearts will be warm at the thought of old Ireland
When we're in the green fields of Amerikay.

From "The Green Fields of Amerikay"
Traditional Ulster song, nineteenth century

It's goodbye Mick and goodbye Pat and goodbye
	Kate and Mary
The anchor's weighed, the gangway's up,
I'm leavin' Tipperary!
There's the steamer blazin' up,
So I shall no longer stay.
And I'm off to New York City boys,
Three thousand miles away, HA HA HA!!

From "Leavin' Tipperary," traditional Irish song, 19ᵗʰ century

Now the Kellys run the statehouse and the Kellys
	run the banks
The police and fire departments sure the Kellys
	fill the ranks
Dan Kelly runs the railroad, John Kelly runs the seas,
Kate Kelly runs the suffragettes and looks
	right good to me.
Well I went and asked directions from a naturalized Chinee
And he said, but please excuse me, for me name it is
	Kell Lee.
And there's Kelly from Dublin, Kelly from Sligo,
Little Mickey Kelly who came from County Clare.
Sure Kelly built the pyramids with good old
	Galway granite,
And when Kelly discovered the North Pole
Didn't he find Pat Kelly there.

Irish-American vaudeville song, 1920s

Goodbye Murshee Durkan, for I'm sick and tired
   of workin',
No more I'll dig the praties, and no more will I be fooled.
For as sure as my name is Kearny, I'll be off to Californee,
Where instead of diggin' lumps of dirt,
I'll be diggin' lumps of gold!

From "Mursheen Durkan,"
Traditional Irish song, 19[h] century

The Prince of Camelot

The Kennedy name is legendary in the United States. The assassinations of President John Fitzgerald Kennedy and his brother Robert, and the unexpected deaths of JFK Jr., and his wife in a plane crash were cause for international mourning. I had the honour to travel with Robert Kennedy's 1968 Presidential campaign as a foreign correspondent.

By Dave Abbott

Landing at Seattle's SeaTac airport was uneventful but we could hear the chanting of Bobby's name, even before the engines shutdown.

As we taxied into position we could see the many welcoming signs —We Love You Bobby! Bobby for President; RFK for President — displayed like news headlines over waving and chanting crowds.

"Bob-bee, Bob-bee, Bob-beee, Bob-beeeeee," the two syllable word rose like a wave of sound over the tarmac, bouncing off the nearby hangers before returning to meet another wave. The effect was awesome.

When the 707 American Airlines private jet came to a standstill, the plane quickly emptied as the cameramen and reporters scrambled for an advantageous position on the tarmac to record the arrival of the Prince of Camelot, Robert F. Kennedy.

I delayed my exit, preferring to watch as 'Bob-ee' prepped for public view. He had the body of a high school athlete, neat, trim, not a scrap of superfluous fat, like a bantamweight fighter with a wry toughness you couldn't miss. He wasn't as handsome or as polished as Jack, but he had the look, the look of his brother but in spades -- that mysterious star quality that made him stand out -- the bright blue eyes, the compact wiry body that exuded almost-visible waves of energy.

His hair was longer than I'd expected and he held a mirror in his left hand combing his teenager quiff repeatedly to make sure it was just right. Catching my reflection in the mirror, he smiled at me shyly like a schoolboy. Before turning to leave he paused and asked

"You're new on board, aren't you?

I nodded.

"Where are you from?"

"I'm from Canada but I'm Irish" I replied.

"So am I, he said, " as you might have heard. We must talk later."

"May the wind be at your back," I said and smiled.

He smiled in return. "Are you coming?" he inquired and without waiting for a reply stepped outside. The wind immediately caught the carefully coiffed hair and tousled it.

I waited a while before catching up with him on the tarmac, tucking into his right shoulder as we entered the covered walkway lined with people pushing and chanting, five to ten deep on both sides.

There was no security, no bodyguards, no Rosie Greer or Rafer Johnson protecting him. He was completely vunerable, yet he had many enemies dating back to when he was attorney-general in JFK's administration. He'd savaged Jimmy Hoffa and the International Teamsters Union, pursued organised crime, tried to eradicate Fidel Castro (including the Bay of Pigs fiasco) and had a reputation as a vindictive son-of-a gun.

It was also likely that assorted racists and fanatics were waiting for a chance to eliminate another Kennedy granting them instant infamy. One right-wing Bible Belt magazine had even issued a call to arms with a headline which screamed "RFK Must Die!"

Yet here he was plunging recklessly into the crowds with total disregard for his own safety. Larry O'Brien later explained that Bobby didn't want anyone to think he feared being shot the same as his brother, so he did some pretty dumb things.

His personal style was to reach out to people and to place as few obstacles as possible between himself and the crowd. He neither liked or didn't have much faith in the Secret Service -- after all what had they done for Jack ?

I later learned his office received dozens of threatening letters and telephone calls each month and that the FBI had warned him of "copycat" murders. But he continued to travel in open-topped cars, even though his brother had been murdered in one, and would not tolerate plainclothes bodyguards separating him from the multitudes.

Around us were hundreds, mostly young and black, reaching out to touch his hem, with a kind of supplication more commonly associated with the Pope. The adoration was primitive, simple and from the heart. A touch from Bobby conferred healing and renewal. This was no public relations exercise in mass hysteria.

As the photographer for Life magazine had earlier said to me, "Bobby is not manicured. Bobby is Bobby. He's real." The crowds pressing so close were also real and considered even more demonstrative than they had been for Jack and Jackie. We had difficulty making progress. Outside the terminal thousands more waited as we struggled towards the black limousines lined up at the sidewalk. They grabbed for Bobby's hair, reaching for his jacket, pulling on anything belonging to him. He always wore cufflinks, but they'd been torn off his shirt long before. His hands were already covered with scratches from people reaching for him, scraping him with watches, rings and fingernails.

We reached the open doors just before the crowd surged forward and we sped away from the curb, with the Stars and Stripes flags fluttering on either side of the limousine's hood.

All traffic on the freeway was halted so we arrived at the University of Washington campus unimpeded.

The U of W Hec Edmundson Pavilion, home of the Huskies Basketball team, is a typical college gymnasium. But that day it was transformed into a gigantic fraternity house for a party. Thousands of students, the largest gathering in the history of the university, were waiting to meet RFK.

Balloons, hats, horns, dozens of "Down with the Draft" signs ringed the balcony side-by-side with lifesize pictures of Bobby. An effigy of LBJ, portraying him as a murdering Uncle Sam, hung from the girders.

The dress was straight Haight Ashbury, tie-dye shirts,

105

granny dresses and no bras. It looked like a Laura Ashley convention but for the pungent smell of marijuana wafting and eddying in swirls in the rafters of the floodlit gymnasium.

A volcanic roar greeted Bobby's arrival. The floorboards were quaking as we squeezed through ranks of cheering students to the speaker's podium. From my position I studied his body language, watching him brush his unruly hair and the crinkle in his blue eyes as his boyish smile lit up the room. He punctuated the air with his hands, that being one of the defining physical attributes of Bobby.

His star quality and speech cadence and inflection were more seductive than Elvis'. He didn't just speak, he emoted. His distinct Boston accent commanded silence as he shared his feelings, openly, voicing his beliefs with passionate sincerity. It was a masterful riveting performance, and the students cheered his every line.

Leaving the arena was a terrifying experience. The intensely hyped-up students threatened to overpower us as we struggled towards the exit. I stayed close to Bobby, acting as a bodyguard, warding off the hands and arms reaching to touch him, holding onto his belt to snake him through the crush of bodies.

Once we had reached the safety of the university security men, who'd cleared a passage to the line of waiting limousines, I recall thinking, "If anyone wanted to kill Kennedy it would be very easy right now."

It was not a profound thought.

He was shot dead by Sirhan Sirhan ten days later.

Irish Toasts

Traditionally, toasts in Ireland have a spiritual dimension, or they are gently amusing. The common toast is "slainte" which has numerous meanings, including "welcome," hello, good health and cheers. Many of these toasts are very old and are translated from the original Gaelic into English.

Here's to you and yours
and to mine and ours.
and if mine and ours
Ever come across to you and yours,
I hope you and yours will do
As much for mine and ours
As mine and ours have done
For you and yours!

♣

May those who love us love us.
    And those that don't love us,
May God turn their hearts.
    And if He doesn't turn their hearts,
May he turn their ankles,
    So we'll know them by their limping.

Here's to a long life and a merry one.

A quick death and an easy one.

A pretty girl and an honest one.

A cold beer – and another one!

Here's to our wives and girlfriends:

May they never meet.

♣

When we drink, we get drunk.

When we get drunk, we fall asleep.

When we fall asleep, we commit no sin.

When we commit no sin, we go to heaven.

So, let's drunk and go to heaven!

♣

May your glass be ever full.

May the roof over your head be always strong.

And may you be in heaven

Half an hour before the devil knows you're dead.

May you live as long as you want,

 And never want as long as you live.

Here's to the land of the shamrock so green,

 Here's to each lad and his darlin' colleen,

Here's to the ones we love dearest and most

 And may God bless old Ireland,

That's an Irishman's toast.

♣

We drink to your coffin,

 May it be built

 From the wood

Of a hundred year old oak tree,

 That I shall plant tomorrow.

♣

As you slide down the bannister of life,

 May the splinters never point the wrong way.

Health and long life to you.
   Land without rent to you.
   A child every year to you.
And if you can't go to heaven,
   May you at least die in Ireland.

   ♣

Here's to health, peace,
   and prosperity;
May the flower of Love
   never be
Nipped by the frost
   of disappointment,
Nor the shadow of grief
   fall among
Your family or friends.

   ♣

I drink to myself
   and one other
And may that one other
   be he
Who drinks to himself and one other
   and may that one other be me!

Olde Erin's Proverbs

Proverbs are intended to be considered and thoughtful. Irish proverbs frequently sound like fun or deeply spiritual, neither of which may be necessarily true, but command our attention nonetheless. It is therefore important to approach each one with a smile and a tolerance normally reserved for your grandmother.

A silent mouth is melodious.

♣

The truth comes out when the spirits go in.

♣

However long the road there comes a turning.

♣

A friend's eye is a good mirror.

♣

Who keeps his tongue keeps his friend.

♣

There is no fireside like your own fireside.

♣

When mistrust comes in, Love goes out.

Good resolutions are merely cheques that men draw on a
bank where they have no account.

♣

If you do not sow in the spring you will not reap in the
autumn.

♣

If you want to be criticized, marry.

♣

Instinct is stronger than upbringing.

♣

It is not a secret if it is known by three people.

♣

A lock is better than suspicion.

♣

Need teaches a plan.

♣

The light heart lives long.

Blessings

The Irish are big on blessings. They bless you not just when you sneeze, but upon greeting you, upon saying farewell and certainly if you have just bought them a pint. Many of these blessings are still used today as a matter of speech throughout the country. Try using them—they usually bring a smile in return.

May the road rise to meet you.
May the wind be always at your back.
    May the sun shine warm upon your face.
And the rains fall soft upon your fields.
    And until we meet again,
May God hold you in the hollow of His hand.

          ♣

Always remember to forget
    The things that made you sad
But never forget to remember
    The things that made you glad.
Always remember to forget
    The friends that proved untrue.
But never forget to remember
    Those that have stuck by you.

114

Always remember to forget the troubles that passed away.
But never forget to remember
The blessings that come each day.

♣

May the saddest day of your future be no worse than the
happiest day of your past.

♣

May you have warm words on a cold evening,
A full moon on a dark night,
And the road downhill all the way to your door.

♣

May you live to be a hundred years
With one extra year to repent.

♣

May the Lord keep you in His hand
And never close His fist too tight.

♣

May your neighbours respect you,
Trouble neglect you,
The angels protect you,
And heaven accept you.

May the Irish hills caress you.

    May her lakes and rivers bless you.

May the luck of the Irish enfold you.

    May the blessings of Saint Patrick behold you.

♣

Bless your little Irish heart

    And every other Irish part.

♣

Long may you live

    And may smoke always

Rise from your roof.

♣

May your right hand always

    Be stretched out in friendship,

But never in want.

    May the ten toes of your feet

Always steer you clear of misfortune.

♣

May the roof above you ne'er fall in,

    And your friends gathered below never fall out.

The Last Word

Every Irishman wants the last word, especially if it really is his last. Epitaphs are therefore very important and must not be written in a cavalier fashion. The words must be chosen carefully in order to resonate for centuries. Start writing your own now.

Beneath this stone like clay
They buried him today;
He lived the life of Riley
While Riley was away.

♣

Here lies
The body of
Lt. Col. MacMahon
Accidentally shot
By his Batman
While cleaning
His rifle.
"Well done
Thou Good and Faithful Servant."

Here lies the body of James Shaw
    who came to Mullingar
    and died for the benefit of his health.

♣

He didn't smoke or drink or swear,
    Or go out with the girls.
    Too bad!
Nor did he live to be 100 years,
    He only felt he had.

A Poem for Christy's Mother

By Dave Abbott

The first time I saw Christy Brown I didn't know it was him. I mean, I didn't even know his name.

The sound of two boys, their voices raised in anger, had caught my attention as I rode my bicycle home from school, taking a short-cut through a Dublin Council Estate.

"Jayzus, will ye keep yer arms in or I'll burst you!"

"Sit still ye little fecker!"

Their ire was directed at a rusty go-car which they were pulling, their voices sounding cheerless among the rows of gray houses with their stark slate roofs which patterned the housing estate.

The ancient contraption with its rickety wheels had seen better days and its occupant looked like a rag doll. But as I came closer, I could see the head of a boy poking out over the edge of the makeshift pram. He was clearly helpless, his head lolly-gagging from one side to the other as the cart bumped over the cracked pavement.

The council estate was only a few years old but already most homes housed more children than had been intended. Many had families like Mrs. Brown's, who had given birth

119

to 22 children. Only thirteen survived infancy.

Christy was Mrs. Brown's tenth child, and his had been a most difficult birth. He was four months old before his mother understood there was something wrong with him. His head had a habit of falling backwards whenever she tried to feed him.

The doctors diagnosed Christy as a spastic and suggested that he be placed in a special residential school for those with cerebral palsy. She refused to consider such a thing. "Christy belongs at home with the other kids," she said, and that ended the debate.

Her attitude was most unusual, for her husband was a low-paid bricklayer, dependent on seasonal employment, and with eleven mouths to feed in an overcrowded house, money was short.

But Mrs. Brown remained adamant — Christy would stay home. She would look after him, nurse him, encourage him and slowly, patiently, agonisingly he would learn to read, write type and paint with the toe of his left foot, as he later recounted in his best seller *Down All the Days*.

With the help of his family, especially his mother and Dr. Richard Collis, he overcame his physical disability, which concealed the imaginative and sensitive mind that made him an international celebrity.

I met Christy for the first time when writer Ulick

O'Connor introduced us. Christy was 34 at the time and had just moved into his newly built bungalow with a motorised wheelchair and a wealthy American wife.

He was now a bona fide star. His poetry was passionate and resonated with the young and old of Ireland. His writing was considered Joycean and his paintings much sought after, especially in America.

My interview with him for the Canadian Broadcasting Corporation was difficult for both of us. For me because I knew his words might prove impossible for the Canadian listener to understand; for him because he wanted so desperately to speak and enunciate clearly.

I asked him: "Is this a book about Dublin's slums?"

"No," he answered. "It's about ordinary houses where ordinary people lived and loved. An ordinary place. It's what I saw and experienced. It's what I saw and felt."

As he spoke his head and hands were constantly on the move, hands combing the air, as if fighting off unseen demons in an effort to express himself.

"Are you worried that as a result of your success that, like Brendan Behan, you might lose something of yourself?"

His head rolled. His neck stiffened. His fingers gripped the arms of the high-tech cart and he held himself rigid.

"No. I hope not. I don't think so. What you have you have, no matter what happens or where you're from or who you meet. What you have you always have. Whatever that is."

Then Ulick O'Connor, in his lovely soft Dublin accent, read aloud Christy's favourite poem, which he had written for his mother.

Only in your dying, lady, could I offer you a poem.
With gay uplifted finger you beckoned
And faltering I followed you down paths I would not
Otherwise have known and heard.
Leaping after you up that secret mountain
Where you sang without need of voice or words.
I touched briefly the torch you held and bled
Pricked by a thorn from the black deep rose of your courage.
From the gutter of my defeat of dreams
You pull me to heights almost to your own.
Only in your dying, lady, could I offer you a poem.

After the interview, when we'd had a couple of large whiskeys, he called me a "gobshite" and roared with laughter as he told me to "feck off." He was having a grand time.

Christy Brown died in 1981. He was 49.

Daniel Day Lewis won an Oscar playing Christy in Noel Pearson's Production of "My Left Foot."

About the Author

For years the lilting Irish voice of Dave Abbott has delighted radio listeners, television viewers and live audiences on four continents. He has been a broadcast columnist, writer, media executive and an acclaimed public speaker.

Born in Dublin he moved to Canada and became involved in the lively radio talk show scene for a number of stations in Vancouver and Victoria, and for a television talk show in Vancouver.

The world is Dave's beat. He has travelled the globe from South Africa to Tuscany; Ireland to Hong Kong; throughout China and his beloved Canada.

Dave is a travel writer, a lecturer for Holland America Cruise Lines and the host and producer of Asia Pacific Diary on the DenTV Network (www.dentv.com). He is also the host/producer of Celtic Voices (www.fm961.com) on radio and Celtic World on TV.

Glossary

Cead mile failte :   one hundred thousand welcomes

Codger : an old man

Colcannon : mashed cabbage and potatoes

Josser : an old Irish man

Craic : repartee, verbal gymnastics, word play

Cumallyis : stories and songs from the country

Gargle : a drink

Seannacai : story teller

Slagging : verbal gymnastics

Slainte : welcome

Stocious : drunk

Tir-na-Og : land of the forever young

Index

Order Form

YES! Please send me the following order of *Catch the Irish Laughter.*   **14 SENNOK CRES.**
VANCOUVER, B.C.
V6N 2E4 CANADA

Number of Copies at $17.95 each   _____

Shipping and Handling:
Please add $2.00 per copy $_____

TOTAL ($19.95 per book) $_____

Name _____

Address _____

City _____

State/Prov. _____ Zip/Postal Code _____

Enclosed is my check/money order for $ _____
Please bill my
VISA ④ MASTERCARD ④   AMERICAN EXPRESS ④

Account No._____

Expiry Date _____

Signature _____